What is the Torah?

A **BE KY** Book

Hollisa Alewine, PhD

DEDICATION

To Alan, who has always been my greatest encourager.

CONTENTS

INTRODUCTION

What is the Torah? If you're reading this booklet, then very likely you've begun to hear friends or family using the word, and it's also likely that you're not Jewish. Maybe you've wondered why this Jewish word keeps coming up in conversations when it would be so much simpler to call the Scriptures by the name familiar to most Christians: *The Holy Bible*.

This booklet explains why it is helpful to refer to a specific section of Scripture as the Torah, for understanding many difficult passages in the New Testament, or even the Prophets and Psalms of the Old Testament, depends upon understanding the place of the Torah as the "Law of Moses" in its historical context. For instance, why does Jesus tell the woman at the well that "Salvation is of the Jews"?

The Jews have guarded and kept the Torah for thousands of years, and Zechariah prophesies of a time when righteous people from the nations will seek out a Jew for direction in finding their way to Jerusalem, the Holy City.

> '...So many peoples and mighty nations will come to seek the LORD of hosts in Jerusalem and to entreat the favor of the LORD.' Thus says the LORD of hosts, 'In those days ten men from all the nations will grasp the garment of a Jew, saying, ""Let us go with you, for we have heard that God is with you.'"[1]

1. Zechariah 8:22-23

Perhaps looking at the ancient Scriptures from Jesus'

very Jewish point of view will explain his statement concerning salvation and Zechariah's prophecy of unity in spiritual direction between Jew and Gentile.

With that general direction in mind, our objectives are to:

- Define the Torah.
- Define the nature of the Torah.
- Identify to whom the Torah is given and in whom it is sealed.
- Establish that the new commandment is not old, but "from the beginning," Genesis 1:1.
- Explain that the Torah is for the process of perfecting the "whole" House of Israel: all those who hold fast to the commandments of the covenant and Sabbaths.
- Identify Jesus as the embodiment of the Living Word
- Recognize the need to yield the human body as a lamp for the great light of the spiritual Torah.
- Define and identify equivalent expressions: Torah, commandment, statute, precept, ordinance, Word, testimony, light, lamp.
- Identify thematic connections between the older and new testaments.

GLOSSARY

Adonai – my Lord.

Brit Chadasha – New Testament. In Hebrew, literally, "Renewed Covenant." The Hebrew word for new, *chadash*, also means renewed, as we apply the adjective to the New Moon. The moon is not new; it is the same moon. Its appearance is merely renewed each month. By the same token, Jeremiah 31:31 defines the terms of the New Covenant: the Torah will be written on the hearts of God's people. It is not a new Torah, but the old Torah renewed in a dynamic way because of the work of Yeshua, a better mediator than Moses.

Chok(im) – ordinances of the Torah which have no rational explanation; the only explanation is that "you are to be holy for I am holy."

Equivalence of expression – an equivalent expression will explain a certain expression of the compared word or phrase. It is not exactly the same, but equivalent in essence. It may be a metaphorical definition or descriptor.

Hermeneutics – Methods of Biblical interpretation applying accepted rules of interpretation.

Menorah – a lampstand, specifically, the 7-branched golden lampstand that stood in the Holy Place of the Tabernacle and Temple.

Mishnah – the Jewish oral law traditionally believed to have been passed down from Moses. Yeshua usually upheld the oral law of the House of Hillel, but he overruled most of the oral laws of the House of Shammai. They were the two predominant schools of the Pharisees in the First Century. His method of determining the validity of oral law was to judge whether it set aside a written commandment in favor of the traditions of men.

Mishpat(im) – judgments. The mishpatim often deal with ethical or moral laws; they are logical and the rationale behind them is easy to understand.

Moed(im) – alludes to seasons and the appointed feasts of Israel: Passover, Unleavened Bread, Firstfruits of the Barley, Firstfruits of the Wheat (Pentecost), Trumpets, Day of Atonement, and Tabernacles

Nefesh – the bundle of appetites, desires, emotion, and intellect.

Rebbe/Rabbi – a Jewish spiritual leader or teacher.

Talmud – the largest body of Jewish law and commentary containing the Mishnah, Gemara, and Tosefta.

Tanakh – Old Testament. Tanakh is an acronym for Torah, Neviim, Ketuvim, or Law, Prophets, and Writings, the ancient divisions of the Hebrew Bible. The books of the Tanakh are the same as, but are not arranged in the same order as Christian Bibles.

Torah – the first five books of the Bible, misunderstood as "law" in English translations. The Torah is more accurately God's teaching and instruction. It contains topics such as science, history, priestly procedures, civil statutes, ordinances, health, agriculture, commandments, prophecies, prayer, animal husbandry, architecture, civics, and many others. The root word of Torah comes from the Hebrew word *yarah*, which means "to hit the mark." Torah may also be used to refer to all of the Hebrew Bible, or even to its smallest meaning, a procedure. Torah may be used by Messianic Jews to refer to the entire Bible from Genesis to Revelation, for the Torah is the foundation for all the Scriptures. The Prophets point Israel back to the Torah. The Psalms teach one to love the Torah as King David loved it. The Writings teach the consequences of departing from the Torah and the rewards for returning to it. The New Testament brings the Torah to its fullest meaning in the person Yeshua the Messiah, and much of the New Testament quotes the Tanakh.

Yeshua – Jesus' Hebrew name; salvation.

1

WHAT IS THE TORAH?

Torah is a word that many people know, but not everyone understands what it means. Admittedly, the word Torah has more than one meaning, so it is helpful to know the context in which it is being used and by whom. Briefly, the written Torah is defined as:

a. hitting the mark, as with an arrow
b. teaching and instruction
c. first five books of the Bible
d. foundation of the entire Bible (most scholars agree it is directly or indirectly quoted 350 times in the New Testament

The Strong's number is H8451 (tow-rah'), and it is derived from the root ya-rah, Strong's H3384, which is defined as:

a. to throw, cast
b. to cast, lay, set
c. to shoot arrows
d. to throw water, rain

Unfortunately, many English translations of Torah render it as "law," which is a limited translation of the

Hebrew word. The root word of Torah, *yarah* is often used in the Older Testament, and the root is not rendered into "law," but words like "teaching" (most often) and shooting arrows to hit the mark accurately. Interestingly, the plain meaning of Torah is directed instruction, but it also denotes "prophetic instruction and instruction in the Messianic age"[2] according to the Lexicon. As if to reinforce the positive meaning of Torah, the word Torah is mentioned most frequently in the Book of Psalms, the most encouraging of books. The word Torah is mentioned 35 times in the Psalms.

The Book of Proverbs gives an example of the gentler aspect of Torah, which connotes a kindly teacher, not a jailkeeper or judge:

> My son, observe **the commandment** of your father; and do not forsake the **teaching (Torah)** of your mother (Proverbs 6:20)

The Torah also means the first five books of the Bible: Genesis, Exodus, Leviticus, Numbers, and Deuteronomy. The Hebrew names of the first five books are based on the first word or phrase in the individual book. For instance, *Bereishit* (Genesis) literally translates to: "In the beginning..."

By the time the New Testament was written, the Torah was also referred to as "Moses":

> Then beginning with Moses and with all the prophets, He explained to them the things concerning Himself in all the Scriptures. (Luke 24:27)

Yeshua's (Jesus') explanation of his ministry to his disciples in reference to "Moses" also included teaching from "all the Prophets" and "all the

2. http://bit.ly/ 1RdVsjL

Scriptures." While Christians refer to this collection of books as the Old Testament, Jews call this same collection the TANAKH, which is a Hebrew acronym of:

> **The Law (Torah)**
> **The Prophets (Neviim)**
> **The Writings (Ketuvim)**

While the books are identical in both Christian and Jewish Bibles, the organization of the Prophets and Writings sections following the Torah is a little different. Sometimes if a Jewish person says, "Torah," he means the entire TANAKH, or Old Testament.

One reason for this may be that all the Prophets pointed Israel back to the Torah for repentance (return to God), and the Writings, such as Psalms, demonstrated to Israel how to love the Torah as King David, a prophetic picture of Yeshua. The Old Testament, or TANAKH, is the Scriptures that Yeshua and the Early Church used to preach the Gospel.

Although it's easy to see how much of the New Testament directly quotes the TANAKH because many translations put the quotes in all capital letters, most scholars agree that either directly or indirectly, it is referenced in 85% of the New Testament. For Hebrew-reading or speaking Jews who study the TANAKH faithfully, the hints in the New Testament are easy to identify.

As an example of a hint to a Hebrew-speaking person who knows that the root of Torah is *yarah*, hitting the mark with an arrow, the Apostle John speaks of a white horse rider in Revelation Six who carries a bow that shoots arrows. The Hebrew word for both bow and rainbow is the same. An arrow in

Hebrew is *chetz*, meaning "to divide."

Thus the reader has two pictures that connect to the Word of God, the Torah. The arrow is like a sword, which the Revelation red horse rider carries. The sword, *cherev*, is a sharp instrument that has the spiritual connotation of "rightly dividing the Word of Truth," but its Hebrew root, *charav* (H2717), is "to dry up."

> And take...the sword of the Spirit, which is the Word of God. (Ephesians 6:17)

> For the word of God is living and active and sharper than any two-edged sword, and piercing as far as the division of soul and spirit, of both joints and marrow, and able to judge the thoughts and intentions of the heart. (Hebrews 4:12)

These two plagues of bow and sword are judgment on those who defy the Word of God in Revelation, and they allude to the same thing: the Torah, God's teaching and instruction. While human beings can judge one's compliance with the Word of God on the outside, only the Spirit of God can judge a love of the Torah on the inside.

In the concluding words of the Torah, Moses warned the Israelites that the Torah should be welcomed like the dew on thirsty grass; likewise, in the concluding message of the New Testament, the Apostle John warns Yeshua's disciples that the Word should still be welcomed like dew on thirsty grass or judgment is coming on those who make no effort to hit the mark of the Father's instruction or to drink up the dew of the Word. Yeshua also rides a horse in judgment:

He is clothed with a robe dipped in
blood, and His name is called The
Word of God. (Revelation 19:13)

The apocalypse prophesied by Moses for departing
from the Word of God in Deuteronomy is echoed by
John's apocalypse. He declares the end from the
beginning. The white horse rider carries a crown in
addition to the bow. Yeshua also returns on a white
horse:

And I saw heaven opened, and
behold, a white horse, and He who sat
on it is called Faithful and True, and in
righteousness He judges and wages
war. His eyes are a flame of fire, and
on His head are many diadems; and
He has a name written on Him which
no one knows except Himself. (Rev
19:11-12)

Is this another Hebrew hint to the Torah?

Gird Your sword on Your thigh, O
Mighty One, in Your splendor and Your
majesty! And in Your majesty ride on
victoriously, for the cause of truth and
meekness and righteousness; let Your
right hand teach (yarah) You
awesome things. Your arrows are
sharp; the peoples fall under You; Your
arrows are in the heart of the King's
enemies. (Psalm 45:3-5)

The themes once again are connected: kingship,
sword, arrows, judgment, and teaching of the Word.
For the seeker of truth and righteousness, it is a
beautiful picture of the returning Messiah, who
teaches the Word of God, and it validates the thirst
of those who accept His Word like dew. For the

King's enemies, their rejection of the Word draws a
sharp arrow.

2

EQUIVALENCE OF EXPRESSION

In both Christian and Jewish hermeneutics[3], there is a similar interpretive technique called "equivalence of expression." An equivalent expression will explain a certain expression of the compared word or phrase. It is not exactly the same, but equivalent in essence. It may be a metaphorical definition or descriptor. Walter C. Kaiser, Jr.'s, academic texts on Biblical exegesis are good sources that explain how to detect equivalent expressions. An explanation and example of how to apply an equivalent expression is found in Appendix A.

It is important to read the entire passage for context, for another rule of Biblical exegesis is that "context is everything." A rule that is common to both Judaism and Christianity is the Rule of Complete Mention. This involves compiling all the contexts in which a particular word or phrase appears and then comparing them for a thematic thread of meaning. In Judaism, the rule is called *Davar hilmad me'anino* (Explanation obtained from context). The total context, not just the isolated statement, must be considered

3. Methods of Biblical interpretation applying accepted rules of interpretation

for an accurate exegesis.

Explanation obtained from context is related to the Christian method of Complete Mention. A good way to use this method is to use a concordance to search on the word. It will list all uses of the word in the Bible. Reconciling TANAKH and New Testament (*Brit HaChadashah* – New Covenant) words is a little more advanced because a Greek word may have a Hebrew equivalent. However, read each usage in context. If there is a consistent use and definition of a word that holds true through most of the text, then the expressions may be equivalent.

When it comes to Torah, however, the equivalent expressions are incredibly easy to find. The Father did not want His children to struggle with His Word, and if anything is important to the Father, it must be for His children to learn His instructions so that they can hit the mark effectively. While sometimes the examples are scattered throughout the Scriptures, often they are found within the same chapter or verse:

> For He established a testimony in Jacob and appointed a law (Torah) in Israel, which He commanded our fathers that they should teach them to their children, that the generation to come might know, even the children yet to be born, that they may arise and tell them to their children, that they should put their confidence in God and not forget the works of God, but keep His commandments...The sons of Ephraim were archers equipped with bows, yet they turned back in

the day of battle. They did not
keep the covenant of God and
refused to walk in His law (Torah).
(Psalm 78:5-10)

Bows shoot arrows of the spiritual Torah: to the
wicked, the arrows' trajectory is to judgment; to
the righteous, the Torah of the testimony of
Yeshua has a trajectory intended to heal.

In Psalm 78 above is a familiar cluster of related
words. Proverbs 6:20 established that the Torah
was something related to a mother's teaching:
"My son, observe **the commandment** of your
father; and do not forsake the **teaching (Torah)** of
your mother." Within that same verse, the
commandment of the father is linked to the torah
of the mother.

The Ten Commandments specify that one is to
honor his father and mother, for they are two, but
they are one flesh. The father demonstrates the
sterner aspect of the Torah, the commandment,
but the mother demonstrates the nurturing
aspect of the teaching. There are benefits to
obedience and consequences for disobedience
to the commandments of Adonai. This applies to
both young and old children: children of earthly
parents and children of the Father above.

We have a good list of related words:
commandment, Torah, works of God, testimony.
As you read more references, add them to the
list.

WORD OR EXPRESSION	VERSE REFERENCE
commandment	Psalm 78:5-10; Proverbs 6:20
Torah	Psalm 78:5-10; Proverbs 6:20
testimony	Psalm 78:5-10

works of God	Psalm 78:5-10

Examine the following passage, and add more equivalent expressions to the preceding chart:

> O how I love Your law (Torah)! It is my meditation all the day. Your commandments make me wiser than my enemies, for they are ever mine. I have more insight than all my teachers, for Your testimonies are my meditation. I understand more than the aged, because I have observed Your precepts. I have restrained my feet from every evil way, that I may keep Your word. I have not turned aside from Your ordinances, for You Yourself have taught me. How sweet are Your words to my taste! Yes, sweeter than honey to my mouth! From Your precepts I get understanding; therefore I hate every false way. Your word is a lamp to my feet and a light to my path. (Psalm 119:97-105)

The Psalm reinforces the actual definition of the Torah: teaching and instruction. The Psalmist weaves in the metaphor of Torah as a teacher, declaring that it gives him more insight than a teacher of earthly things. There is a passage in Galatians that also alludes to the teaching essence of the Torah:

But before faith came, we were
kept in custody under the law,
being shut up to the faith which
was later to be revealed.
Therefore the Law (Torah) has
become our tutor (paidagōgos) to
lead us to Christ, so that we may
be justified by faith. But now that
faith has come, we are no longer
under a tutor. For you are all sons
of God through faith in Christ
Jesus. (Galatians 3:23-26)

The Lexicon entry for *paidagōgos* reads:

A tutor, i.e. a guardian and guide
of boys. Among the Greeks and
the Romans the name was
applied to trustworthy slaves who
were charged with the duty of
supervising the life and morals of
boys belonging to the better class.
The boys were not allowed so
much as to step out of the house
without them before arriving at the
age of manhood.

*Vines Expository Dictionary of New Testament
Words*, however, contrasts the work of the
teacher (Torah) with the tutor in these specific
verses:

Here the idea of instruction is
absent. In this and allied words the
idea is that of training, discipline,
not of impartation of knowledge.
The *paidagogos* was not the
instructor of the child; he exercised
a general supervision over him
and was responsible for his moral

and physical well-being. Thus understood, *paidagogos* is appropriately used with 'kept in ward' and 'shut up,' whereas to understand it as equivalent to 'teacher' introduces an idea entirely foreign to the passage, and throws the Apostle's argument into confusion." [Notes on Galatians, by Hogg and Vine, pp. 163, 164]

Paul describes the written Torah as ethical guidelines to keep a person safe until his maturity. When he is "grown" in the spiritual Torah, he can function independently. The student under the tutor has no choice, but the student who has actually learned and internalized the spirit of the instructions has become them. He obeys the commandments of the Teacher without compulsion, as Yeshua said, "If you love me, keep My commandments." Paul's explanation is clear when compared with the Psalmist's, for the one who has loved the commandments because he loves the Father has indeed exceeded a teacher who only taught the ethics of the Torah without the Spirit of the Torah, which is characterized by love.

An example of this is the process schoolchildren undergo when they learn math. A first grade teacher teaches the students that $1 + 1 = 2$. After this information is internalized and used, the formula is less "counted" and more "known." The student no longer needs the teacher as a guide to impute the information. When the child reaches the point that he or she simply sees two things and perceives $1 + 1 = 2$ without having to analyze the data, the information is a part of the child. It becomes part of who the child is, not what he counts. The first grade teacher passes into the child's memory, but the information never changes. The child intrinsically knows what the exterior presents.

Psalm 119:97 declares, "O how I love Your law (Torah)!" It sets the foundation for the statements that follow it in context. Within that context, there are several equivalent expressions:

> • **Commandments**
> • **Your testimonies**
> • **Your precepts**
> • **Your word**
> • **Your ordinances**
> • **Your words**

There is room in the chart to add the new equivalents. An equivalent expression will explain a certain expression of the compared word. It is not exactly the same, but equivalent in essence. It is a metaphorical definition or descriptor. For example:

> These commandments that I command you today...You shall write them on the doorposts of your house and on your gates. (Deuteronomy 6:6-9)

> **doorposts ≈ gates**

Both words represent an opening to a dwelling, both literal and spiritual, so they are equivalent expressions, one small, one large.

Your word is a lamp to my feet and a light to my path. (Psalm 119:105)

For the commandment is a lamp and the teaching (Torah) is light; and reproofs for discipline are the way of life... (Proverbs 6:23)

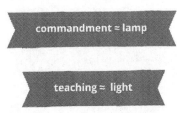

The commandment focuses the light of the Torah in a human being, so the Torah as light is greater, diffuse and intangible, but the Torah in a human being becomes a lamp. Although smaller, the lamplight is more practical and useful in the created world.

As for the mystery of the seven stars which you saw in My right hand, and the seven golden lampstands: the seven stars are the angels of the seven churches, and the seven lampstands are the seven churches. (Revelation 1:20)

John to the seven churches that are in Asia: Grace to you and peace, from Him who is and who was and who is to come, and from the seven Spirits who are before His throne (1:4)

stars ≈ angels (messengers) of the seven churches

seven lampstands ≈ seven churches

Him who is and who was and who is to come ≈ Seven
Spirits before the throne

This is where it is important to be careful in applying equivalence of expression. Used loosely, one might be tempted to say that the seven churches **are** God, which would be foolish. However, the equivalence is demonstrating relationship among the things listed. If the Spirit is in the seven churches, then the seven churches are a lampstand on the earth, just as Yeshua was a lampstand. A disciple of Yeshua takes that which is spiritual, His Word, obeys that Word in love, and then he or she becomes a light to others. A star, like a lamp, is even more visible in darkness.

Another word cluster emerges in these verses from Revelation and Proverbs 6:23:

Torah
Word
Commandment
Seven Spirits of God
Seven Assemblies

Each of these words relates in some way to the seven-branched menorah (lamp). Using whole contexts, it is easy to see that the Father never intended his Word merely to be the tutor, but the teacher of His children. He wants His children to apprehend the spiritual relationship to His Word along with the physical. Indeed, the Living Word Yeshua stated:

If you love Me, you will keep My commandments. (John 14:15)

Jesus answered and said to him, 'If anyone loves Me, he will keep My word; and My Father will love him, and We will come to him and make Our abode with him. He who does not love Me does not keep My words; and the word which you hear is not Mine, but the Father's who sent Me. These things I have spoken to you while abiding with you. But the Helper, the Holy Spirit, whom the Father will send in My name, He will teach you all things, and bring to your remembrance all that I said to you.' (John 14:23-26)

This sounds much like Psalm 119, emphasizing the Holy Spirit as the Teacher of the Word. When the disciple forgets the Word, then the Spirit can remind him and teach him all things. Ironically, the Hebrew way to say "things" is *devarim*, which is the fifth book of the Torah, Devarim (Deuteronomy). After the Psalms, Deuteronomy is the book that most mentions the Torah. It mentions it more than any other book of the Torah itself. Yeshua renders a play-on word, for in Hebrew, *devarim* means both "Words" and "things."

The Torah is something that requires the work of the Holy Spirit in order to make an individual a desired abode for the Father and His Son. It is quite evident when an individual lives a life apart from the Word, but it is also evident when an individual obeys the Word without the Spirit, and the Father cannot make a home there.

3

BUT AREN'T JESUS' COMMANDMENTS NEW ONES, NOT THE OLD ONES?

Good question. Yeshua would not leave so important a question unanswered. Children who are loving disciples of the Word would never settle for the forced obedience to a tutor; they would desire to keep the Father's commandments because of a loving relationship. John writes to believers Yeshua's wishes:

> My little children, I am writing these things to you so that you may not sin. And if anyone sins, we have an Advocate with the Father, Jesus Christ the righteous; and He Himself is the propitiation for our sins; and not for ours only, but also for those of the whole world. By this we know that we have come to know Him, if we keep His commandments. The one who says, "I have come to know Him," and

does not keep His commandments, is a liar, and the truth is not in him; but **whoever keeps His word, in him the love of God has truly been perfected.** By this we know that we are in Him: the one who says he abides in Him ought himself to **walk in the same manner as He walked. Beloved, I am not writing a new commandment to you, but an old commandment which you have had from the beginning; the old commandment is the word which you have heard. On the other hand, I am writing a new commandment to you, which is true in Him and in you, because the darkness is passing away and the true Light is already shining.** (1 John 2:1-8)

Because children often misunderstand, the language in which John writes is plain and loving. The Word is to be the foundation of action in a loving relationship between the Father and His sons and daughters. That action is modeled after the way that Yeshua walked, without blame in reference to the Torah. Yeshua walked according to the "old commandment...from the beginning."

But did he? As an equivalency clue, John plants the phrase "from the beginning." *Bereishit* ("In the beginning...") is the first word of the Torah. Is that the only significance to the "beginning"? Keep reading, and in Genesis 1:2, the Father identifies what was moving even before the physical creation obeyed His commandments:

...and the Spirit of God was moving over the surface of the waters. Then God said, 'Let there be light'; and there was light. God saw that the light

was good; and God separated the
light from the darkness. (Genesis 1:2-4)

The Torah is a light, and the commandment is a
lamp. In the beginning, the will of *Elohim* [4] was to
have a people who would walk in His Spirit,
separating light from darkness in loving obedience to
His commandments. The Book of Romans is replete
with the interplay between the Torah of God and the
torah of the flesh. The Torah of the Father is a Light,
and His commandment is a lamp, but the teaching
of the flesh is darkness, and its ways lead to sin and
death:

> Thanks be to God through Jesus Christ
> our Lord! So then, on the one hand I
> myself with my mind am serving the
> law of God, but on the other, with my
> flesh the law of sin. (Romans 7:25)

The Torah of the Creator is not a new
commandment, but an ancient Word. However,
John writes, "On the other hand, I **am** writing a new
commandment to you, which is true in Him and in
you, because the darkness is passing away and the
true Light is already shining." How can John say the
commandment is old and new at the same time?

Through the work of Yeshua, the commandment is
new and fresh through the Spirit of Messiah that was
moving on the surface of the waters. The Spirit stirs,
the commandment goes out, and the Word is seen in
the physical world, a world confused in darkness and
separated from the Light of the Torah. When the
Light shines, the Creation is reminded that life is found
in obedience to its Creator. This is the true light,
commandment-keeping inspired of the Spirit.

Keeping the commandments of the Creator only with
the flesh does not bring light, but when it is the Holy

4. First name of
God used in
Scripture as the
Creator.

Spirit that moves in these clay vessels to become lamps, the physical Creation shines in obedience!

As if to reassure Yeshua's faithful, John writes again concerning the commandment "from the beginning":

> Now I ask you, lady, not as though I were writing to you a new commandment, but the one which we have had from the beginning, that we love one another. And this is love, that we walk according to His commandments. This is the commandment, just as you have heard from the beginning, that you should walk in it. For many deceivers have gone out into the world, those who do not acknowledge Jesus Christ as coming in the flesh. This is the deceiver and the antichrist. (2 John 1:5-7)

John makes an additional point. Yeshua came in the flesh. Although Messiah was the Word of Spirit "in the Beginning" (John 1), he came into the Creation as a physical being. To deny that Messiah is both Spirit and flesh is to deny the Gospel, which is that Messiah did come in the flesh to save the souls of all, Jew and Gentile. To make him only a spiritual being would negate the physical resurrection of Messiah. To make him only a man is again to negate the spiritual Word, who was Messiah Yeshua. It takes both to proclaim the Gospel.

In like manner, to proclaim a physical commandment apart from the Spirit is to strip its essence and leave a meaningless shell. It is a shell that will quickly disintegrate when the tutor looks the other way. To make the commandments only

Spiritual is to deny that it takes works of obedience along with the Spirit for there to be life in the commandment. Faith without works is dead.

For instance, if I have been married for many years, but one day I tell my husband, "Honey, my spirit is really in love with you, but with my body I want to be with this other man..." then how long can that relationship endure? We love our spouses with spirit, soul, and body. It is an exclusive relationship that grows because we learn what pleases the other. We attribute value to that covenant partner, not another, and we consider the needs and desires of the other, not merely our own.

It is the same in commandment-keeping. It is a meeting place where an individual can know the will of the Bridegroom and learn to grow in what pleases Him. There is no way the relationship will thrive if I make that relationship only spiritual, and with the body I serve the desires of my own flesh. To do so would be to deceive myself and walk in a spirit of anti-messiah. This would be a terrible abuse of a great gift of both Spirit and flesh to mankind.

THE TORAH IS THE MENORAH IN YOU!

For the commandment is a lamp and the teaching (Torah) is light...(Proverbs 6:23)

Teaching, teaching, teaching...yes, this is the message of the Torah. It is not just any teaching, but the instructions of the Father so that His children may be identified with Him. But haven't we heard people say that no one can keep the law?

We've all had experience putting together those items that said, "Some assembly required," but the instructions seemed completely unrelated to the actual pieces and hardware in the kit! Apart from the obvious problem of the Creator purposely giving instructions that He knew His children were incapable of following, think about what teaching and instruction actually implies. It implies we're all in the learning process. Well, Hallelujah!

Yeshua never commanded his disciples to perfectly keep the Torah; he commanded them to be disciples. A disciple is a student, someone learning. A disciple never stops learning. Grace is sufficient when one's learning or motivation falls short, which it surely will. Take careful note of Yeshua's instructions about the "light of the world":

> You are the light of the world. A city set on a hill cannot be hidden; nor does anyone light a lamp and put it under a basket, but on the lampstand, and it gives light to all who are in the house. Let your light shine before men in such a way that they may see your good works, and glorify your Father who is in heaven. Do not think that I came to abolish the Law (Torah) or the Prophets; I did not come to abolish but to fulfill. For truly I say to you, until heaven and earth pass away, not the smallest letter or stroke shall pass from the Law (Torah) until all is accomplished. Whoever then annuls one of the least of these commandments, and teaches others to do the same, shall be called least in the kingdom of heaven; but whoever keeps and teaches them, he shall be called great in the kingdom of heaven. (Matthew 5:14-19)

Yeshua doesn't say everything is already fulfilled. If so, we would already be sporting those righteous robes. However, Yeshua does say it is important both to learn and to teach the commandments of the

Light, the Torah. It is something for which to strive with the power of the Holy Spirit until Yeshua returns. Until then, just like the ancient Israelites, the Torah is righteousness "for you."[5] It is not your righteousness, [6] but Yeshua's. You are simply walking in the steps he walked before you from the foundation of the world. The righteousness does not originate from the individual, but from the Seven Spirits of Messiah (Isaiah 11:1-2) [7] that He leaves with His children to teach them.

5. Deuteronomy 24:14

6. Although there are verses of Scripture that state the righteous man will be rewarded, the Jewish view is that even the totally wicked have some characteristics of righteousness; for instance, King Herod was fascinated with the Essenes, a strictly-observant religious sect. However the Jewish way of looking at this is that the wicked are rewarded for their righteousness in THIS world, but for those who take on the righteousness of God, the reward is in the world to come. This is not to be confused with the blessings inherent in obeying the Word in this life.

7. For a more thorough study of the Seven Spirits of Messiah working through the Creation, the Seven Feasts of Israel, and the Seven Churches of Revelation, see the author's Creation Gospel Workbook One: The Creation Foundation.

5

DIGGING DEEPER

This study of the Torah has so far focused mainly on Scriptures that can be found in any Sunday School New Testament, which usually contains the Books of Psalms and Proverbs. There is more richness to be found in digging deeper into the TANAKH and the foundations of the Newer Testament. The Torah itself states:

> For this commandment which I command you today is not too difficult for you, nor is it out of reach. It is not in heaven, that you should say, 'Who will go up to heaven for us to get it for us and make us hear it, that we may observe it?' Nor is it beyond the sea, that you should say, 'Who will cross the sea for us to get it for us and make us hear it, that we may observe it?' But the word is very near you, in your mouth and in your heart, that you may observe it. (Deuteronomy 30:11-14)

The Torah reinforces the equivalent expressions:

commandment and Word. If some measure of the Spirit of God is within each individual, which is what differentiates a human being from a beast, then even the most wicked person has a spark within that yearns toward the Word of God. It is in every heart, but whether that spark of Light is cultivated depends upon the decisions of the individual heart. What that individual hears, says, and plans in his heart as seed grows works from either of two realms: the realm of the carnal flesh, like a beast, or from the realm of the Spirit above, which is the image in which man was created and intended.

> Behold, days are coming,' declares the LORD, 'when I will make a new covenant with the house of Israel and with the house of Judah, not like the covenant which I made with their fathers in the day I took them by the hand to bring them out of the land of Egypt, My covenant which they broke, although I was a husband to them,' declares the LORD. 'But this is the covenant which I will make with the house of Israel after those days,' declares the LORD, 'I will put My law (Torah) within them and on their heart I will write it; and I will be their God, and they shall be My people.' (Jeremiah 31:31-33)

The New Testament, or New Covenant, is frequently seen as something brand new in Adonai's plan for man. In Hebrew, however, new does not always mean completely new, but renewed. For instance, the Hebrew month is *chodesh*, and the time of month when the moon is new is *rosh chodesh*. But is it a brand new moon, or is our perspective of it new? The Hebrew words used for New Covenant, *Brit Chadasha* (Strong's 1285 & 2319), specify that the principle of covenant relationship will continue.

The word *chadasha* means "new or fresh." From the context, Jeremiah is speaking of a refreshing of the covenant. It is not the Torah that will change, but the hearts of His People. The relationship of husband and wife is used to demonstrate the attraction of the heart to the Word of the covenant. Ezekiel also speaks of this new covenant heart, adding that the Spirit is what will make the difference:

> For I will take you from the nations, gather you from all the lands and bring you into your own land. Then I will sprinkle clean water on you, and you will be clean; I will cleanse you from all your filthiness and from all your idols. Moreover, I will give you a new (*chadash*) heart and put a new (*chadashah*) spirit within you; and I will remove the heart of stone from your flesh and give you a heart of flesh [8]. I will put My Spirit within you and cause [9] you to walk in My statutes, and you will be careful to observe My ordinances. You will live in the land that I gave to your forefathers; so you will be My people, and I will be your God... Ezekiel 36:24-28

8. Flesh is *basar*, which also spells the same word *basar*, "good news," a synonym for the Gospel.

9. *Asah*, which means to do, to accomplish, or to make. The fresh heart is fashioned by the Holy Spirit.

It is one thing to be filled with the Holy Spirit, but according to the foundation of the Prophets, what is the Spirit put within a man to do? The Holy Spirit within a man's heart yearns toward the spiritual commandments of his Father, or as Jeremiah wrote, it yearns like the attraction of a faithful spouse to her husband.

(statutes) and
mishpatim
(ordinances) is
an interesting
juxtaposition of
two categories
that are
subgroups of
the Torah. The
Torah would be
the all-
encompassing
group, but
categories
within the
whole are
statutes,
ordinances,
commandment
s, precepts, etc.
Chukim,
according to
the rabbis,
have no basis in
logic; they are
to be obeyed
out of pure
loyalty and
faith that the
Holy One knows
best; the
mishpatim are
more legalistic
and logical.
Ezekiel's choice
of words implies
a heart that
obeys even
before it
understands as
well as a heart
that sees the
moral and
ethical basis for
the instructions.

In fact, the attraction and power of love is so strong that the Spirit impels the People of God to walk in His "ordinances and statutes" [10] carefully, which are the finer details of the Torah. Wow! With the power and the teaching of the Holy Spirit, covenant life with the old commandment is full of fresh life, for just as John wrote, it is a new commandment as well as old!

Still in context of a return to the Covenant and Torah, Ezekiel prophesies of future flocks of men, which Christians readily identify as the "other sheep" that he intended to gather:

> Thus says the Lord GOD, 'This also I will let the house of Israel ask Me to do for them: I will increase their men like a flock. Like the flock for sacrifices, like the flock at Jerusalem during her appointed feasts, so will the waste cities be filled with flocks of men. Then they will know that I am the LORD.' (Ezekiel 36:37-38)

Ezekiel speaks specifically about Jerusalem and her "appointed feasts" (*moedim*) and their role in gathering these future flocks of people who attach to the covenant of Israel in the freshness of the Spirit. Although observant Jews are diligent to gather at the appointed feasts of Israel, many Christians have not yet seen the need; however, as the Torah is written on their New Covenant hearts by the Spirit, expect those multitudes of sheep to have a heart-change toward the feasts of Israel. They will gather at the appointed times of Passover, Pentecost, and Tabernacles.

Yeshua came to save souls. In Hebrew, a soul is a *nefesh* (plural *nafshim*). The simplest definition of a *nefesh* is that it is the bundle of appetites, desires, emotion, and intellect. The soul is housed in the body, similar to an animal, but the Spirit of Elohim (God) breathed into the human being distinguishes him from a beast. Clean beasts are often used to symbolize the souls of men in Scripture, for it is always clean beasts that are required for sacrifice, not wild beasts. In this way, it represents the substitution of the sacrifice for the man, the animal's required perfection representing the perfection that the man's soul hopes to attain through the Spirit.

While the spirit of a man comes from God and will return to Him (Ecclesiastes 12:7), his soul is corrupted in his carnal flesh. The part of a man that yearns toward the Torah of Elohim is his spirit, and the spirit is like the flame of a candle that bends and reaches for a nearby flame. It is the body and soul of earthly desires that pull the man toward the earth, a place of decay and death once the spirit returns to Elohim.

Sometimes the words "soul" and "spirit" are used in error by those who don't read Hebrew, and it is an honest mistake for English-speakers, for a quick check in a concordance reveals how many other English words are used to translate a word such as *nefesh*. For instance, sometimes it is translated as the word "person." While a person has a soul, if the Scripture wished to emphasize a person's soul as the focus of its message, then it makes sense to look up those words in a concordance if one is reading a translation from the original language.

Paul points out what Ezekiel established, that the observance of the Torah is the result of a spiritual renewal. The spirit man yearns toward the Torah, which is holy, righteous, and good. The Torah, however, exposes the parts of the heart that are still earthbound to the desires of the soul. The Torah exposes sin for what it is:

So then, the Law (Torah) is holy, and the commandment is holy and righteous and good. Therefore did that which is good become a cause of death for me? May it never be! Rather it was sin, in order that it might be shown to be sin by effecting my death through that which is good, so that through the commandment sin would become utterly sinful. For we know that the Law (Torah) is spiritual, but I am of flesh, sold into bondage to sin. (Romans 7:12-14)

The spiritual Torah/commandment separates the truth of the spirit from the sinful flesh and "restores (repents) the soul." An individual must come to repentance, and this is the salvation that Yeshua, the Living Word, offers both Jew and Gentile. This is the "new Spirit" of the Torah foretold by Ezekiel, a Holy Spirit that can restore the soul's affection for the spiritual commandments of the Torah.

The law (Torah) of the LORD is perfect, restoring the soul; the testimony of the LORD is sure, making wise the simple. (Psalm 19:7)

Yeshua came to attach his disciples to the commandments of the Torah with sacrificial love. This frees the spirit from the bondage of the body and soul that holds the man captive. The soul and body are intimately joined. The soul is captive in the body, but the body is captive to the desires of the soul. The Torah "breaks" the authority of the soul over the spirit, which in turn releases the spirit of man from captivity to his appetites, desires, emotions, and intellect.

Instead, the soul begins to hunger for things of the

Spirit, desire the will of the Father, emote the truth of the Spirit, and think the thoughts of the Father. Yeshua came to bring the refreshing Spirit that could restore those who desired to return to the authority of the Holy Spirit over their hearts and to let the Father's Word train their souls to submit to the Truth of the Spirit; the Word is Truth.

6

ISN'T THE TORAH ONLY FOR JEWS?

Thankfully, the Torah isn't only for Jews! In fact, every commandment in the Torah is not for everyone. There are man commandments, woman commandments, child commandments, priest commandments, government commandments, farmer commandments, merchant commandments, property commandments...you get the picture. There are only a certain number of commandments that can apply to any given individual, but certainly, observant Jews keep more of the Torah than Christians. On the other hand, most Christians freely keep more commandments than the Big Ten, such as tithing, not raping, abstaining from bestiality, and many others.

Many Christians are beginning to keep the appointed feasts of Israel, such as Ezekiel mentioned, as well. The Spirit is beginning to write some "new" things on the hearts of the sheep from another fold:

> Let not the foreigner who has joined himself to the LORD say, 'The LORD will surely separate me from His people.' Nor let the eunuch say, 'Behold, I am

a dry tree.' For thus says the LORD, 'To the eunuchs who keep My sabbaths, and choose what pleases Me, and hold fast My covenant, to them I will give in My house and within My walls a memorial, and a name better than that of sons and daughters; I will give them an everlasting name which will not be cut off.
(Isaiah 56:3-12)

Do you see the equivalent expression in the first verse?

Foreigner ≈ Eunuch

What does a foreigner have in common with a eunuch? Neither has the hope of covenant offspring, for the foreigner, although allowed to reside within the borders of Israel, was forced to live under the laws of Israel:

One law shall be to him that is homeborn, and unto the stranger that sojourneth among you. (Exodus 12:49 KJV)

One law and one manner shall be for you, and for the stranger that sojourneth with you. (Numbers 15:16 KJV)

His offspring, however, were not considered part of the covenant community, for demanding his compliance with the precepts of Torah was primarily to prevent him from tempting Israelites to transgress the Torah. For instance, a Gentile who opens his shop on Sabbath tempts the native-born Israelite to transgress the Torah and lose the beautiful Spirit of rest in Messiah on the Shabbat (Nehemiah 13).

In order to be admitted into the congregation of Israel, the stranger, like Ruth, needed to voluntarily decide to become part of the community. Although Modern Judaism would call this a conversion, in ancient times the process was less formal. The stranger was expected to go beyond the ethical commandments, called Noachide [11] laws, and to embrace the full covenant of Israel out of love. To this group of people Isaiah directs his prophecy. Those who formerly had no share in the covenant and Kingdom would be given a place even better than natural-born sons and daughters. The native-born would not have to fight so much adversity to learn the written commandments, but for the one "brought near," it would be a struggle.

A "name" in Scripture is one's deeds as much as the actual written or spoken name. It is one's reputation for doing. When a stranger is guaranteed a "name that will not be cut off," it is an assurance that his or her deeds of the Spirit, the result of Torah written on the heart of flesh, will be remembered. What a promise to the righteous stranger! [12] Isn't this what Paul assures the Ephesians in Chapter Two, that they have been brought near to the Covenant through the blood of Yeshua?

Keeping the Sabbaths of Israel, which includes both the weekly Shabbat and the special sabbaths of the appointed feasts, is an outward sign of a changed heart that is no longer a stranger to the Torah. Isaiah continues his encouragement to Gentile believers:

> Also the foreigners who join themselves to the LORD, to minister to Him, and to love

11. Orthodox Judaism has defined the Noachide laws as: Do Not Deny God, Do Not Blaspheme God, Do Not Murder, Do Not Engage in Incestuous, Adulterous or Homosexual Relationships, Do Not Steal, Do Not Eat of a Live Animal, Establish Courts/Legal System to Ensure Law Obedience. The Tosefta (Av. Zar. 8:6) records four possible additional prohibitions against: drinking the blood of a living animal, emasculation, sorcery, and all magical practices listed in Deuteronomy 18:10–11.

12. A "stranger" in Hebrew has two connotations, and within modern Judaism, the ger tzedek "righteous Gentile" is a convert to Judaism. Another word for non-Jew is goy, which can simply mean a non-Jew, someone from "the nations."

the name of the LORD, to be His
servants, every one who keeps from
profaning the sabbath and holds fast
My covenant; even those I will bring to
My holy mountain and make them
joyful in My house of prayer. Their burnt
offerings and their sacrifices will be
acceptable on My altar; for My house
will be called a house of prayer for all
the peoples. (Isaiah 56:6-7)

Yeshua quotes this very verse when he overturns the
moneychangers' tables in the Temple! The
moneychangers were part of a sect of the Pharisees
known as "The House of Shammai." According to
their doctrine, a Gentile had no part in the World to
Come no matter how righteous he was. Shammai
refused to teach Gentiles the Torah. The House of
Shammai made it practically impossible for a Gentile
to become Jewish and worship the God of Abraham,
Isaac, and Jacob even though it was prophesied
that Abraham and Sarah would be mother and
father to many nations.

Frequently the Shammaite moneychangers would
funnel the funds from Gentiles who sent or brought
Temple sacrifices into the pockets of politically
appointed Temple officials. Yeshua rejects this
doctrine and states unequivocally that room should
be made for the stranger to draw near. He doesn't
just hint to Isaiah's welcoming words to the righteous
Gentiles, he quotes him. One of the first things a
believing Gentile would do is observe the Shabbat,
resting on the Seventh Day, and observing the
appointed feasts of Israel, for repeatedly Israel is
warned in the Torah to welcome the stranger, alien,
orphan, and widow at those times.

Gentiles in Scripture denote either an uncircumcised
pagan or someone who is not a Jew or Israelite by

birth. The first application is negative, but not the second one. The first is rooted in the individual's behavior, but the second is rooted in his ethnicity, which is his Creator's choice. A person's spiritual behavior is his or her own choice.

A righteous Gentile, according to Paul's epistles, is not a pagan, but one learning the Torah with the sensitivity of the Holy Spirit. He appreciates its teaching and instruction for Godly living, following the footsteps of Yeshua. He is a child making a name in the Temple of Jerusalem above like a natural-born son or daughter.

In his epistle to the Galatians in Chapter Four, Paul compares those who received the Torah at Mount Sinai to Hagar and inferior to those who are like Sarah and Jerusalem "above." What does he mean? In brief, Hagar was a slave. Her role within Abraham's family was forced upon her. Sarah, however, was the loved one, a gift of the Father to Abraham and the recipient of the promise to be a mother of many nations. Sarah represents those who have a willing covenant relationship to the Father, for her relationship to Abraham was one of love. Scripture even says she called him "Lord," out of reverence.

After the Israelites received the Torah at Mount Sinai, however, they behaved like Hagar, worshiping a golden calf. They called the image the Name of the Father, made up their own feast day, and celebrated it. Like Hagar, a slave will quickly revert to soulish instead of spiritual behavior. A person with the Torah written on his heart is in a love relationship to the Word. This is a true Child of Israel, the offspring of Sarah, not a mocking Ishmaelite offspring of the bondwoman Hagar. Isaac was the child who internalized the teaching of his father Abraham, for in Genesis 26:5, the Holy One tells Isaac that he will inherit the promise of his father "because Abraham obeyed my voice, and kept my charge, my commandments, my statutes, and my laws."

Don't we all want to be the "love children" of our father Abraham and our Heavenly Father?

> Bind up the testimony, seal the law (Torah) among my disciples. And I will wait for the LORD who is hiding His face from the house of Jacob; I will even look eagerly for Him. Behold, I and the children whom the LORD has given me are for signs and wonders in Israel from the LORD of hosts, who dwells on Mount Zion. When they say to you, 'Consult the mediums and the spiritists who whisper and mutter,' should not a people consult their God? Should they consult the dead on behalf of the living? To the law (Torah) and to the testimony! If they do not speak according to this word, it is because they have no dawn (shachar). (Isaiah 8:16-20)

Isaiah mentions more words from the cluster of equivalent expressions: Torah, testimony, word. He even mentions the "children." The Torah is something that is sealed among the disciples, or students of Torah. In fact, Isaiah says, if they don't speak according to the testimony and word of Torah, they have no "dawn." What does he mean?

Throughout Scripture are parables. A parable helps human beings to apprehend spiritual concepts, which can't be seen, by using physical objects and places, which can be seen. For this reason some prophecies seem anachronistic, for in one generation may come prophecies against many kingdoms, such as Tyre, Assyria, and Babylon. Each king represents some aspect of the parable, and as an example, the King of Babylon is addressed both in Isaiah as well as Revelation. Babylon can be described as both male and female, for it is a parable. In Revelation, Babylon is described as "fallen, fallen." This is a thematic connection to two important passages of Scripture. In Isaiah, the parable is addressed to the King of Babylon:

> How you have fallen from heaven, O star of the morning, son of the dawn (shachar)! You have been cut down to the earth, you who have weakened the nations! But you said in your heart, 'I will ascend to heaven; I will raise my throne above the stars of God, and I will sit on the mount of assembly (moed) in the recesses of the north. I will ascend above the heights of the clouds; I will make myself like the Most High.' (Isaiah 14:12-14)

The aspiration of the King of Babylon, who once was a "son of the dawn," was to ascend a throne above the mount of the moed. This alludes to the "appointed feasts" to which the flocks of men would gather with Spirit-filled hearts for the Torah. When he was a "star of the morning, son of the dawn," the King of Babylon was an obedient servant. When he desired to rise to the throne and rule over the holy, spiritual feasts, however, he fell. Now Yeshua, the obedient servant, is the "morning star." He is restoring all people, Jew and Gentile, to the mount of the moed, gathering the Father's flocks of sheep. Yeshua doesn't want to ascend above the "stars of God," he wants to MAKE stars of God, shining lights in the darkness as John wrote about in Revelation. Because authority is derived from obedience, the Father gives Yeshua all authority to sit on the throne beside Him, for he sacrificed his own life to draw in the righteous Gentiles from their weakened state among the nations. He came to gather them into the clouds to himself, just as the Angel of the Presence in the cloud was given the authority of the Name to protect and lead the Israelites in the wilderness; indeed, both "women" are taken to the wilderness in Revelation.

John's and Isaiah's apocalyptic prophecies have something in common: they reiterate the need for light to separate from darkness by recognizing spiritual authority. They acknowledge the Morning Star. The Torah is a light, and the commandment is a lamp. And "I, Jesus, have sent My angel to testify to you these things for the churches. I am the root and the descendant of David, the bright morning star." [13] If one wants to understand the seven seals of Revelation, it is as simple as following the Scriptural clues from the Torah, through the Prophets, through the Writings, through the Gospels, and to the Book of Revelation.

> ...who also sealed us and gave us the Spirit in our hearts as a pledge. (2 Corinthians 1:22)

> In Him, you also, after listening to the message of truth, the gospel of your salvation—having also believed, you were sealed in Him with the Holy Spirit of promise... (Ephesians 1:13)

> Do not grieve the Holy Spirit of God, by whom you were sealed for the day of redemption. (Ephesians 4:30)

Isaiah assured readers of his prophecy that the disciples of Yeshua had both the Word and the testimony sealed in them. If not, they had no "dawn," which is associated with the Morning Star,

13. Revelation 22:16

48

Yeshua. When the seven seals of Revelation are opened, it is the Holy Spirit that seeks the wicked for destruction, yet it seeks the righteous for their final gathering:

> Have you ever in your life commanded the morning, and caused the dawn to know its place, that it might take hold of the ends of the earth, and the wicked be shaken out of it? It is changed like clay under the seal; and they stand forth like a garment. (Job 38:12-14)

Gentile and Jewish believers who have the dawn of the Torah sealed in their hearts know their place, and it is in covenant with the Word of God. They are clay changed under the seal of the Holy Spirit, and their changed hearts are being revealed. On the other hand, the imprint of a seal reveals two things: that which yields to the pressure of the writing and that which resists and stands forth. The same Torah reveals both the student of the Word the one who resists it.

7

TYING IT ALL TOGETHER: SPIRIT, SOUL, BODY

Modern Torah scrolls are often bound in linen and tied or secured with a sash. In the same way, human beings are like little Torah scrolls. The tablets of the commandments given to Moses were written front and back. Like the clay under the seal, what was inscribed was both concealed and revealed. The scroll with the seven seals in Revelation is likewise written front and back.

Each believer in Yeshua will have commandments written on the exterior. Some will have more written than others, for they have been learning and practicing longer. What really matters, though, is what is written on the INSIDE of the scroll, what is sealed in the heart. In the Messianic Kingdom, the Torah will go forth, and the teaching and learning will continue:

> And many peoples will come and say,
> 'Come, let us go up to the mountain
> of the LORD,
> To the house of the God of Jacob;

That He may teach us concerning His
ways
And that we may walk in His paths.'
For the law (Torah) will go forth from
Zion
And the word of the LORD from
Jerusalem.
(Isaiah 2:3)

Pay attention to Me, O My people,
And give ear to Me, O My nation;
For a law (Torah) will go forth from Me,
And I will set My justice for a light of
the peoples.
(Isaiah 51:4)

Teaching and learning will continue, but what a
disciple must discern is if the writing on the outside
matches the spirit-man inside, the part of himself that
yearns toward the Spiritual Torah above. If the deeds
don't reflect the internal writing, then something is
amiss. By the same token, if the exterior writing
reflects lots of works of the Torah, but there is no
spiritual transformation within, then again, something
is amiss. Only the Holy Spirit can discern the disparity
between what is revealed and concealed in the
scroll, but when the seals are opened, all things will
be revealed.

The Word of God is full of equivalent expressions,
internally defining and teaching serious students of
the Word what the Torah is. As a review,

> To the law (Torah) and to the
> testimony! If they do not speak
> according to this word, it is because
> they have no dawn. (Isaiah 8:20)

Torah ≈ testimony ≈ word ≈ dawn

The Revelation of Jesus Christ, which God gave Him to show to His bond-servants, the things which must soon take place; and He sent and communicated it by His angel to His bond-servant John, who testified to the word of God and to the testimony of Jesus Christ, even to all that he saw. (Revelation 1:1-2)

Word of God ≈ Testimony of Jesus Christ

So the dragon was enraged with the woman, and went off to make war with the rest of her children, who keep the commandments of God and hold to the testimony of Jesus. (Revelation 12:17)

Commandments of God ≈ Testimony of Jesus

The children who keep the commandments of God and the Testimony of Yeshua are special students sealed with the Holy Spirit of Promise. They are bound in the Torah, but not as unwilling slaves. They are both native-born and strangers [14] brought near because of a refreshed heart. They are in the cloud with Yeshua in the wilderness test; they are stars of witness with Yeshua because they are the seed of Abraham [15]; they have the dawn, for they are learning to separate the Light of Torah from the darkness of sin.

Light is sown like seed for the righteous and gladness for the upright in heart. (Psalm 97:11)

14. "For this reason *it is* by faith, in order that *it may be* in accordance with grace, so that the promise will be guaranteed to all the descendants, not only to those who are of the Law, but also to those who are of the faith of **Abraham**, who is the **father** of us all..."(Romans 4:16). No matter where the stranger is in his sojourning, he is justified by faith in Yeshua, the Word, who is able to bring it to completion, writing on the tablet of his heart.

15. Genesis 15:5

The Torah is a seed of light in the hearts of the righteous. Both righteous Jew and Gentile may walk in the good works of the Torah, for those works originated in the Creator, and we are created in His image. Through the testimony of Yeshua, may we all be sealed in the Torah, works prepared for us so that all we have to do is to learn to walk in them after Him.

> For we are His workmanship, created in Christ Jesus for good works, which God prepared beforehand so that we would walk in them. (Ephesians 2:10)

APPENDIX A

In Judaism, *G'zerah Shavah* (Equivalence of expressions) is an inference or analogy made between two separate texts on the basis of a similar phrase, word, or root. Because the Jewish Oral Law [16] is a comprehensive body of details about the written Torah, the technique usually applies to interpreting the meaning of specific instructions. If the instructions are different in themselves, they are subject to the same application. This sounds more complicated than it is!

The word *gezerah* usually refers to a law (Daniel 4:17) and refers to the comparison of two similar laws. In other words, if the same word appears in two passages, then the meaning applied to one should be also used in the other. Equivalence of expression (*gezerah shavah*) can be abused to make outlandish leaps of logic, so advancing it, whether as a tool used in a Christian seminary or a Jewish yeshiva, should be done with caution. Examples can make it easier to understand:

By comparing 1 Samuel 1:10 to Judges 13:5 using the phrase "no razor shall touch his head," we may conclude that Samuel, like Samson, was a Nazarite [17]. Samson and Samuel were lifetime Nazarites, but we also know that there was provision for those who wanted to take a Nazarite vow for only a specified period of time:

> Now this is the law of the Nazirite: When the days of his separation are fulfilled, he shall be brought to the door of the tabernacle of meeting. Then the Nazirite shall shave his

16. The Mishnah is the oldest collection of Jewish law, which is a practical clarification of how to keep the Torah, which is often terse, telling one to do something, but not how. The Mishnah was passed along orally until the destruction of the Second Temple, and then it was finally recorded in writing. The Talmud developed from additions to and commentary on the Mishnah in later centuries.

17. Numbers Chapter Six details what a man or woman can do in order to enter a period of more intense devotion to God. Briefly, the Nazarite does not cut his hair, nor does he eat or drink grape products. At the conclusion of the vow, the consecrated hair is cut and offered with a sacrifice.

consecrated head at the door of the tabernacle of meeting, and shall take the hair from his consecrated head and put it on the fire which is under the sacrifice of the peace offering. The priest shall take the ram's shoulder {when it has been} boiled, and one unleavened cake out of the basket and one unleavened wafer, and shall put {them} on the hands of the Nazirite after he has shaved his dedicated {hair.} (Numbers 6:13)

By using the equivalence of expression, the reader concludes that Paul actively participated in Nazarite vows for specified periods and brought sacrifices during his ministry. Notably, he continued to do so many years after Yeshua's death and resurrection:

Paul, having remained many days longer, took leave of the brethren and put out to sea for Syria, and with him were Priscilla and Aquila. In Cenchrea he had his hair cut, for he was keeping a vow. (Acts 18:18)

Take them and be purified with them, and pay their expenses so that they may shave their heads, and that all may know that those things of which they were informed concerning you are nothing, but that you yourself also walk orderly and keep the law. (Acts 21:24)

The similarity in actual words, phrases, and themes between Acts and Numbers is the key to drawing parallels between the two passages, linking the Torah with the works of the Paul. The Torah establishes the seed of the Nazirite vow; Samson and Samuel are practical examples of those who are functioning Nazirites; and Paul demonstrates that for those who desire to function in leadership and prophecy, a Nazirite vow was still an (outward) sign of righteousness desired by the individual who followed Yeshua. Paul did not consider either the instructions of Torah or its application a work of self-righteousness, but an act of faith following a spiritual desire for greater faith, for "faith without works is dead." (James 2:17; 26)

Instead of inventing a new way to increase his faith, Paul followed the instructions of the Torah, which "is not an idle word for you; indeed it is your life." (Deuteronomy 32:47) Since Paul identified Yeshua as that Living Word, keeping the Nazirite vow must have been a highly spiritual, not just physical, experience.

QUESTIONS FOR REVIEW

1. Read Deuteronomy 32:1-47 in order to have full context of Moses' speech to the Israelites. Based on the introductory verses, 1-2, explain how the Torah (law) in verse 46 is a good example of Torah's root word, *yarah*.

2. On the chart below is a simple exercise in defining whether Adonai prefers to describe His Torah as a policeman or judge (law), or as an accurate teacher (instruction). On the left side is a column labeled "NEGATIVE - law." The right column is labeled "POSITIVE - instruction." Read Psalm 119 completely and assign each use of the word "law" to one column or the other, depending on how you perceive its use in the text. Use the verse numbers to keep track. In the column labeled "Word Clue(s)," give a word or phrase from the verse that prompted you to assign it to the negative or positive column.

PSALM 119		
NEGATIVE – LAW VERSE #	WORD CLUE	POSITIVE – INSTRUCTION VERSE #
	"how blessed..."	1

3. Read the following verses in Revelation: 1:2, 1:9, 6:9, 19:13, 20:4 3. Do you think the "testimony" and the "Word of God" are different or the same? Explain your answer.

4. Read Deuteronomy 6:6-9 and find all the equivalent expressions. List them below, and then comment on the actual relationship to one another. Are some of them equivalent, yet somehow opposite? Explain.

5. Find the equivalent expressions in the following verse:
Bind up the testimony, seal the law (Torah) among my disciples. (Isaiah 8:16)

Testimony ≈ _____

Bind up ≈ _____

6. A Torah scroll in the synagogue is bound up with linen, covered with a beautifully embroidered mantle, and ornamented with a "crown." How does this symbolize the Living Word, Yeshua? How does it symbolize one of Yeshua's disciples who keeps the Testimony and commandments?

SOURCES TO LEARN MORE

The BEKY Book Series:

www.bekybooks.com

Church History:

Our Hands are Stained with Blood by Michael L. Brown
The Church and the Jews by Dan Gruber
Too Long in the Sun by Richard Rives
Yeshua: a Guide to the Real Jesus and the Original Church by Dr. Ronald Moseley

Hebraic Roots:

The Creation Gospel Workbook Series by Hollisa Alewine
The Feasts of Adonai by Valerie Moody
Torah Rediscovered; Take Hold by Ariel and D'vorah Berkowitz
Paul, the Jewish Theologian by Brad Young
The Complete Jewish Bible translated by Dr. David Stern

Messianic web sources:

www.hebraicrootsnetwork.com
www.thecreationgospel.com

COMING SOON!

More BEKY Books are coming soon. For updates on title releases, go to **www.bekybooks.com**. Here are only a few upcoming topics in this encouraging series:

- Kosher eating
- Biblical feast days
- The Sabbath
- Truth vs Tradition
- Messianic Shabbat Service
- Havdalah
- Yeshua in the menorah
- Pharisees and Yeshua
- Understanding Jewish sources

ABOUT
THE AUTHOR

Dr. Hollisa Alewine has her B.S. and M.Ed. from Texas A&M and a Doctorate from Oxford Graduate School; she is the author of *Standing with Israel: A House of Prayer for All Nations*, The Creation Gospel Bible study series. and a programmer on Hebraic Roots Network. Dr. Alewine is a student and teacher of the Word of God.